A STUDENT'S GUIDE TO
POLITICAL PHILOSOPHY

THE PRESTON A. WELLS JR.
GUIDES TO THE MAJOR DISCIPLINES

GENERAL EDITOR   EDITOR

JEFFREY O. NELSON   JEREMY BEER

PHILOSOPHY *Ralph M. McInerny*

LITERATURE *R. V. Young*

LIBERAL LEARNING *James V. Schall, S.J.*

THE STUDY OF HISTORY *John Lukacs*

THE CORE CURRICULUM *Mark C. Henrie*

U.S. HISTORY *Wilfred M. McClay*

ECONOMICS *Paul Heyne*

POLITICAL PHILOSOPHY *Harvey C. Mansfield*

PSYCHOLOGY *Daniel N. Robinson*

CLASSICS *Bruce S. Thornton*

AMERICAN POLITICAL THOUGHT *George W. Carey*

RELIGIOUS STUDIES *D. G. Hart*

THE STUDY OF LAW *Gerard V. Bradley*

NATURAL SCIENCE *Stephen M. Barr*

A Student's Guide to Political Philosophy

Harvey C. Mansfield

ISI Books
Wilmington, Delaware

The Student Self-Reliance Project and the ISI Guides to the Major Disciplines are made possible by grants from the Philip M. McKenna Foundation, the Wilbur Foundation, F. M. Kirby Foundation, Castle Rock Foundation, J. Bayard Boyle Jr., the William H. Donner Foundation, and other contributors who wish to remain anonymous. The Intercollegiate Studies Institute gratefully acknowledges their support.

Copyright © 2001 Harvey C. Mansfield.

Fourth Printing, August 2006

Cataloging-in-Publication Data

Mansfield, Harvey Claflin, 1932-
        A student's guide to political philosophy/ by
Harvey C. Mansfield. —1st ed. —
        Wilmington, Del. : ISI Books, c. 2001.

        p. / cm. (Student's guide to the major disciplines)
        Prepublication title: A student's guide to political theory

        Includes bibliographical references (p. 55-57)
        ISBN 1-882926-43-9
            1. Political science—Philosophy. 2. Politics. I. Political
        philosophy. II. Title III. Series

JA71 .M36 2001   00-101237
320.01—dc21   CIP

Published in the United States by:

ISI Books
Intercollegiate Studies Institute
Post Office Box 4431
Wilmington, DE 19807-0431

Cover and interior design by Sam Torode

CONTENTS

INTRODUCTORY NOTE

POLITICAL PHILOSOPHY is found in great books—those by Plato, Aristotle, Locke, Rousseau and others of the highest rank—and in books by professors. You should spend much more time with the great authors than with the professors, and you should use the professors to help you understand the great authors; you should not allow yourself to be diverted or distracted from the great books by the professors. Why not go for the gold? Why be content with the dross? I am a professor; so take it from me that I am only a subordinate guide, one with the office of introducing you to the true guides.

Political philosophy can also be found outside the books—in actual politics—but here we see it only in its first strivings, before it appears under its own name. Citizens and politicians do not claim to be philosophers, whom they rather look down on as ingenious but inept. But politics and political philosophy have one thing in common, and that is *argument.* If you listen to the talk shows, you will hear your fellow citizens arguing passionately pro and con with advocacy and denigration, accusation and defense. Politics means taking sides; it is *partisan.* Not only are there sides—typically liberal and conservative in our day—but also they argue against each other, so that it is liberals *versus* conservatives.

PARTISAN DIFFERENCES

EACH SIDE defends its own interests, those of schoolteachers versus those of stockbrokers, for example, but they also appeal to something they have in common: the common good. Defending their interests, each says, contributes to the common good. At the same time, the parties appeal to someone in common, a common judge who would decide the issues between them. Normally this judge is merely the person they are trying to persuade or impress, but he could be a person competent to judge. Arguments, good or bad, are made with reasons and so are aimed implicitly, if not usually, at a reasonable judge. Here is where political philosophy enters. Most people reason badly, but they do reason—and political philosophy starts from that fact. In America today, liberals argue that wealth is unjustly distributed, for example, but they overlook the need to generate wealth. Conservatives do the reverse; preoccupied with wealth generation, they pay little attention to how it should be distributed.

A partisan difference like this one is not a clash of "values," with each side blind to the other and with no way to decide between them. A competent judge could ask both sides why they omit what they do, and he could supply reasons even if the parties could not. Such a judge is on the way toward political philosophy.

There is a long tradition of political philosophy dating from Socrates and consisting of a series of great books, each written to comment favorably or adversely on a contemporary or a preceding philosophy. A scholar can devote his life to this tradition or a part of it, and anyone serious about political philosophy will want to acquire at least some knowledge of the tradition. But one does not have to go to books of political philosophy to find political philosophy. All the books of political philosophy could be lost, if one can imagine such a calamity, and yet the activity could be generated anew directly from political life. The partly rational character of politics calls for completion in political philosophy—even though it takes a great thinker, to whom we are all greatly indebted, to answer the call.

Politics always has political philosophy lying within it, waiting to emerge. So far as we know, however, it has emerged just once, with Socrates—but that event left a lasting impression. It was a "first." I stress the connection between politics and political philosophy because such a connection is not to be found in the kind of political science that tries to ape the natural sciences. That political science, which dominates political science departments today, is a rival to political philosophy. Instead of addressing the partisan issues of citizens and politicians, it avoids them and replaces their words with scientific terms. Rather than *good, just,* and *noble,* you hear political scientists of this kind speaking of *utility* or *preferences.* These terms are meant to be neutral, abstracted from partisan dispute. Instead of serving as judge of what is good, just, or noble, such political scientists conceive themselves to be disinterested observers, as if they had no stake in the outcomes of politics. As political scientists, they believe they must suppress their opinions as citizens lest they contaminate their scientific selves. The political philosopher, however, takes a stand with Alexis de Tocqueville (1805-59), who said that while he himself was not a partisan, he undertook to see, not *differently,* but *further* than the parties.

To sum up: political philosophy seeks to judge political partisans, but to do so it must enter into political debate. It wants to be impartial, or to be a partisan for the whole, for the common good; but that impartiality is drawn from the arguments of the parties themselves by extending their claims and not by standing aloof from them, divided between scientist and citizen, half slave to science, half rebel from it. Being involved in partisan dispute does not make the political philosopher fall victim to relativism, for the relativism so fashionable today is a sort of lazy dogmatism. These relativists refuse to enter into political debate because they are sure even before hearing the debate that it cannot be resolved; they believe like the political scientists they otherwise reject that nothing can be just or good or noble unless everyone agrees. The political philosopher knows for sure that politics will always be debatable, whether the debate is open or suppressed, but that fact—rather welcome when you reflect on it—does not stop him from seeking a common good that might be too good for everyone to agree with.

Political philosophy reaches for the best regime, a regime so good that it can hardly exist. *Political science* advances a theory—in fact, a number of theories—that promises to bring agreement and put an end to partisan dispute. The one rises above partisanship, the other, as we shall see, undercuts it. Now, why should we prefer the former? So far I have argued for political philosophy, but what's wrong with seeking agreement instead of reaching for the moon?

The question is more complicated than we have seen so far, because an important historical fact has not yet been mentioned: political science came from political philosophy. More precisely, political science rebelled from political philosophy in the seventeenth century and in the positivist movement of the late nineteenth century declared itself distinct and separate. The controversy we see now between political science and political philosophy within university departments of "political science" is a consequence of this earlier, deeper rebellion. Today political science is often said to be "descriptive" or "empirical," concerned with facts; political philosophy is called "normative" because it expresses values. But these terms merely repeat in more abstract form the difference between political science, which seeks agreement, and political philosophy, which seeks the best. Political science likes facts because it is thought possible to agree on facts as opposed to values, and political philosophy provides values or norms because it seeks what is best.

When we contrast political science and political philosophy we are really speaking of two kinds of political philosophy, modern and ancient. To appreciate the political science we have now, we need to look at its rival; to do that, we must enter into the *history* of political philosophy. We must study the *tradition* that has been handed down to us. The great political philosophers read the works of their predecessors and commented on them, sometimes agreeing, often disagreeing. This history has less of the accidental in it than other history because, to a much greater degree than citizens or statesmen, philosophers are reflecting upon, and reacting to, thinkers that came before them. In considering the history of Western civilization, one must not forget the tradition of Western thought that inspires and explains the actions of peoples and statesmen. It is both more and less than a tradition in the usual sense—more, as it is more thoughtful, and less, being divided against itself and open to argument and correction. The tradition of political philosophy is not a sequence of customs; still less is it a "canon" established by some dominant political power, as is sometimes said. It is the only tradition that does not claim to be an authority, that on the contrary constantly questions authority; quite unlike the various non-Western traditions, it is not exclusive and not peremptory. It is philosophic. No one can count himself educated who does not have some acquaintance with this tradition. It informs you of the leading possibilities of human life, and by giving you a sense of what has been tried and of what is now dominant, it tells you *where we are now* in a depth not available from any other source.

Much political theory today feels no obligation to examine its history and sometimes looks down on the history of the subject as if it could not be a matter of current interest. But our reasoning shows that the history of political philosophy is required for understanding its substance. The question of what view to take of partisan debate is still an issue today; some people relish their partisanship, some—perhaps a growing number—feel uncomfortable with loud arguments and deplore partisan attitudes. In recent decades the political science profession has been subject to successive new theories such as behavioralism and rational choice, each of which promises to put an end to the old debates over values and to do away with political philosophy. But somehow political philosophy survives, despite efforts to supersede it, just as, despite the failure of those efforts, political science in the modern sense re-emerges periodically to make another try at bringing consensus and doing away with debate. To see what each of them is we must look for their origins.

THE ORIGIN OF NATURAL RIGHT

Cicero, the Roman philosopher and orator (106–43 B.C.), said that Socrates was the first to call philosophy down from heaven, place it in cities and homes, and compel it to inquire about life and morals as well as good things and bad. Here is a precise beginning, together with a definition, of political philosophy. Political philosophy begins with Socrates (470–399 B.C.), who for some reason wrote nothing himself but allowed his life and speeches to be recorded in dialogues written by his students Plato (c. 427–347 B.C.) and Xenophon (c. 430–c. 350 B.C.). Philosophy began before political philosophy; before Socrates there were pre-Socratic philosophers, as they are now known. They studied nature (in Greek, *physis*) and left political and moral matters to professional debaters known as Sophists, who taught rhetoric. One of the Sophists, Gorgias, is portrayed in Plato's dialogue of that name. The rhetoricians taught students to argue both sides of any question, regardless of justice. They assumed, like the pre-Socratic philosophers, that justice is a matter of law or custom (*nomos*), that it has no definition of its own but only reflects the dominating will of a master or ruler.

Socrates did not accept this assumption. He suggested that questions of justice, like those of physics, might admit of answers that are not relative to time or place but are always and everywhere the same. Justice would then not be a matter of convention or *nomos*, but rather of nature or *physis*; there would be a natural justice or natural right. Socrates did not lay it down as truth that there was such a thing. His way was to ask innocent questions such as "What is justice?" The form of the question, What is X? assumes that X has a constant and unchanging essence. Yet justice does seem to vary over time and space, as the relativists of ancient times, as well as those of today, say.

Perhaps the most obvious evidence of natural justice is our belief in it, or rather our belief in *injustice*. This we show whenever we believe we have been treated unjustly, as for example when a student gets a grade that is too low. (Complaints about too-high grades are rare.) When that happens, you do not just shake your head and mutter "that is the way of the world." You get angry, and you do so because you implicitly believe that there really is a justice that does not depend on someone's arbitrary say-so. Anger is a sign of injustice, which in turn is a sign of justice. Anger always comes with a reason; an angry person may not stop to express it, but if he had the time and the ability, he could say why he's angry. That is why, in Plato's *Republic*, Socrates presents us with an alliance between the angry types, the guardians who are compared to dogs, and the philosophers, who do not get angry but calmly ponder the reason of things. Both are involved with justice, the guardians to defend justice and the philosophers to find out what it is. Anger is the animus behind unjust partisanship, as when you wrongly feel you deserve something; but it is also the animus behind just partisanship, when you are rightly incensed. As much as Socrates deplores the anger of a tragic hero like Achilles,

---

PLATO (427–347 B.C.) was born to an eminent Athenian family. After Sparta defeated Athens in 404, a violent oligarchy of "thirty tyrants" came to power in Athens which included several relatives and many friends of Plato's family. The oligarchy was eventually overthrown and democracy restored, but in 399, the Athenian democracy put to death Plato's friend and mentor, the philosopher Socrates, on the charges of irreligion and corruption of the youth. In 388 Plato accepted an invitation from the king of Syracuse to come to Sicily, but he soon returned to Athens and there established a school of philosophy which met in a grove of trees named for a local hero, Academus. The Academy would survive as a major educational institution throughout pagan antiquity.

he does not attempt to squelch anger itself. He does not try to deny fuel to partisanship. Why? Because, it is suggested, the object of anger—justice—is real, not contrived, and good even when it seems to go against your advantage.

The existence, or even the possibility, of natural justice justifies our human, all-too-human partisanship. Even the most indefensibly narrow partisan believes in justice. Though a partisan has only a partial view, he does have that much; he is not totally wrong, and in a sense he means well. Even the Communists and Nazis meant well; they meant to improve humanity. So much for meaning well, you might say! But evil has a finger on the good; though it cannot grasp the good, evil cannot help admitting that the good is superior because that is what even evil wants. Machiavelli, who recommended that we do evil, nevertheless thought this would bring us good. However much we want to resist Machiavelli, let alone the Communists and the Nazis, we also have an argument with them. You cannot have an argument unless you share a concern for some common good, such as justice, about which you are arguing. The possibility of natural justice makes politics interesting; without that, politics is only about winners and losers.

In the *Apology of Socrates* Plato shows Socrates on trial

for his life, accused by his city of not believing in its gods and of corrupting its youth. Socrates gives a speech defending himself and his way of life—a defense of philosophy to non-philosophers who feel threatened by his questioning of political, religious, and family authority. Socrates is intransigent; he refuses to change his way of life, and he provokes his judges in several ways, one of them being an insolent claim that, after he is convicted, his "punishment" should be to be housed and fed in city hall at public expense for the rest of his life. Yet even as he declines to submit, he does condescend nonetheless to give an explanation of the philosophical way of life in terms that his fellow Athenians might understand. He presents himself as having been commanded by the Delphic oracle, or the god Apollo, to find out whether he is in truth the wisest of men, as the oracle is reported to have said. Instead of directly questioning the authority of the god, Socrates uses the god's authority to question the authority of the gods. By this maneuver he seems to deny that he has any subversive intent and claims to be questioning the basis of Athenian society, indeed of all societies— but doing so in the spirit of that very basis. It's as if when the law tells you to obey, it is actually, through the implied reasons for its commands, allowing you to talk back rather than simply obey. No society, not even one as free as ours, can proceed on the assumption that every custom and law is open to question, yet Socrates makes us see that every social practice is indeed questionable. Political philosophy has an elevated character, rising above society by questioning everything, but it also emerges from society when examining its implicit assumptions. In the *Republic*, which records a private conversation rather than a public speech like the *Apology*, Socrates unveils his picture of the best regime, in which philosophers take a break from their somewhat ridiculous and apparently innocuous questioning and become kings. Yet the best regime is nothing but what is demanded by justice as ordinarily understood, at least when we suppose as we often do that someone who knows best ought to be in charge.

The master analyst of partisan politics is Thucydides (C. 460-C. 400 B.C.), whom Jean-Jacques Rousseau called the "true model of an historian." Rousseau explained that Thucydides reported facts of history without judging them, leaving that task to the reader. But the facts Thucydides reports are pregnant with judgments begging to be born. In his *History of the Peloponnesian War*, to be sure, he refrains from offering a picture of the best regime. He shows the best regime to be fatefully divided between Athens and Sparta, the two main opponents in the war, in such manner that the virtues of each city are accompanied by vices and are incompatible with the virtues of the other. Such is Thucydides' noble realism, admiring of greatness in politics and resigned to its limitations.

Yet the deeds of the war that Thucydides relates are illuminated by occasional comment directly from the master—and by speeches of participants invented by the master and reported as if he had been there to take them down. The famous debate between the Athenians and Melians resembles a Platonic dialogue except for the fact that the Melians, having lost the argument, are killed at the end. No Socrates is present to question both sides to uncover the philosophy hidden in their minds, but Thucydides with his marvelous artistry leaves his questions in the speeches and in the

---

THUCYDIDES (C. 460–C. 400 B.C.) was the author of the *History of the Peloponnesian War;* besides this, little is known about him. That war between Athens and Sparta took place from 431 to 404 B.C., in his own lifetime, and he called his history of it "a possession for all time." Thucydides, an Athenian general in the war, was defeated by the great Spartan general Brasidas at Amphipolis in 424, and he was exiled from Athens for twenty years as a result of the loss. Before this, he had caught the plague in Athens (of which he gives so memorable a description in his *History*), but recovered.

speeches' relationship to the deeds, and thus prompts us, without ever urging us, to political philosophy. Partisanship, he seems to say, is based on the notion that we can *choose* how to live; he wants us to reflect also on what one must concede to *necessity*, despite one's wishes.

THE POLITICAL ANIMAL

ARISTOTLE (384–322 B.C.) was a student of Plato's, and he too makes his beginning from partisan politics. But taking a different tack from his teacher, he sets forth in his *Politics* a mixed regime as a more attainable standard than the best regime. He has a best regime of his own, less lofty than Plato's because he staffs it with those excelling in moral virtue rather than philosophic virtue. And in keeping with this difference, he establishes his best regime by degrees (in Books 4 to 6 of the *Politics*), rejecting Plato's drastic measures for going from the ordinary to the best (such as expelling everyone over age ten from the previous society).

The mixed regime is composed of democracy and oligarchy, of the many and the few: these are the two parties to be found, open or hidden, in all societies. Ordinarily, one of these parties dominates and suppresses the other. But

Aristotle notices that each party makes a claim to justice, and this claim can be elicited from its implicit or imperfect expression in partisan speeches and brought out into broad daylight by political philosophy. This is what Plato had done to criticize the ordinary regimes against the standard of the best regime, and thereby to calm the spirits and lower the expectations of zealous youths, such as Socrates' main interlocutors in the *Republic*, Glaucon and Adeimantus. But Aristotle wanted to give such youths something wholesome, yet political, to do; he did not despise moderate improvements in a political situation even though such improvements could not establish the best regime. He compares the political philosopher to a gym teacher who betters the condition of average bodies as well as the best, and who, while leading the exercise of his pupils, also gets some for himself incidentally, as it were. For philosophers live in societies with non-philosophers and can benefit from their societies' being put into sound condition. There is in Aristotle's view something strange about the idea, apparently to be concluded from Plato's beautiful painting of a utopian best regime, that normal life is radically insufficient. For how can what is normal be unhealthy?

A certain degree of political controversy is not only

normal but natural to human beings, Aristotle supposes. He defines man as *by nature* a political animal. But what is a political animal? Other animals are gregarious, bees for example, but they are not political because they do not speak or reason about what is advantageous and harmful, just and unjust, good and bad; they are confined to feeling pain and pleasure. Human beings have to reason about these matters, as they are not perfectly clear. Nature may incline us to what is good, but it does not tell us unambiguously what that is, or move us toward it without hindrance or distraction, as it does with other animals. We humans are by nature political, but there is no single, programmed way of life as with bees. Human nature includes both the freedom and the necessity to construct a regime, for we could not have freedom if nature had done everything for us.

Accordingly, Aristotle says that despite the naturalness

ARISTOTLE (384–322 B.C.) was born at Stagira, the son of a Thracian court physician. As a young man he traveled to Athens to study in Plato's Academy and remained there for two decades. Upon Plato's death he left Athens and was summoned to Macedon to tutor the young Alexander the Great. At about the age of 50, he returned to Athens and established his own school, a friendly rival to Plato's Academy, meeting in a gymnasium called the Lyceum. Aristotle and his students were called "Peripatetics," apparently because they would engage in philosophical conversation while walking.

of politics, we are indebted to the one who first constituted a city or society. To constitute a city one must give it a certain principle or rule for its regime. That principle founds the city and by continually inspiring it, enables it to survive; the principle of rule is held by its current rulers as well as its past founders. One cannot make a city as one can a copper pot, and let it sit there complete, without further human intervention. A political constitution is neither entirely natural nor entirely artificial. If it were entirely natural, there would be only one regime corresponding with human nature: and we would have no freedom to choose the direction of our politics. If it were entirely artificial, we would have no guide for our choice: and the only freedom would be for the first maker, who gets to impose his creation until some other maker comes along.

One must distinguish between what is *by nature*, in which we have no choice, and what is *according to nature*, the standard by which we choose. If there is no single regime imposed on us by nature, what is the regime we should choose that is according to nature? The trouble, again, is that the choice is unclear, because nature seems to give support to both the typical regimes, democracy and oligarchy. Democracy is based on our natural equality, since there are many important respects in which human beings are equal; all have reason, for one. But oligarchy is based on human inequality, for which there is also ample evidence; for instance, the superiority in reason of a few over the many. Which is more important to human life, the fact that all humans have reason, or the fact that they have it very unequally? The answer is not obvious, and the debate continues today even within our democracy as we try to decide what inequalities to allow or encourage within our general principle that "all men are created equal." The choice of a political principle can and will be defended with reasons, but it cannot be secured with a proof sufficiently conclusive to end political debate.

What we choose is what seems best, or is in the interest of those choosing, namely, the rulers—who of course may be the many, that is, the "people" in a democracy. You might ask, why does a choice have to be a principle of rule? Why cannot each person choose for himself without elevating his choice into a principle of rule over others—and thus imposing his will on them? Aristotle's answer is a challenge to our liberal practice of toleration. A choice is not a choice without a reason, he says, but when you give a reason, you say why something is good for you—*and for others like yourself.*

Reason transforms a personal "I" into a more general "we." So Aristotle's dictum that man is a rational animal leads to his definition of man as a political animal who rules himself and others, not one who merely decides for himself only on a whim.

A principle of rule is part rational, part conventional; what is natural has to be completed by what is conventional, and what is conventional has to be guided by the natural. This twofold character of political rule is responsible for the manyness of regimes, and for what Aristotle calls the changeableness of justice. Aristotle is no relativist, but he is also no dogmatist. He is willing to allow that though the justice of the best regime is everywhere the same, justice in the actual regimes we live in varies according to circumstance and convention. One can see that American justice, say, is more democratic than justice in most places elsewhere, and if this is not the justice of the best regime, it is justice in America at present. Every actual political regime has a principle of rule and a way of life that mix nature and convention, reason and unreason. Regimes can be ranked in a hierarchy of good to bad, but in general one cannot ignore the regime and judge matters by a standard of bare or pure morality outside of the context of rule. In sum, if you want to understand politics—anywhere and at any time—you need to know what Aristotle says about the regime.

GODLY POLITICS

FOR THE CHRISTIANS, to whom we now turn, this context is too earthly or this-worldly. To them, the ancient philosophers were pagans, lacking knowledge of, and faith in, the true God. The virtues the pagans praised, described, and studied were laden with attachments to this world, uninspired by faith in the next world; they were nothing but "splendid vices," as Saint Augustine (354–430) might have said (but did not). Before continuing with brief remarks on Augustine and Thomas Aquinas (1225–1274), let me record for this quick trip through the tradition of political philosophy the vital contribution of Cicero (106–43 B.C.).

It was Cicero who kept the tradition alive by enabling it to pass from the Greeks to the Christian world. He brought political philosophy to Rome for a people whose leading lights were gifted in politics and rhetoric but despised anything that derived from the Greeks, whom they had defeated. To them, philosophy smacked of Greek softness. Cicero preserved political philosophy by giving it a

Roman cast in his *Republic,* in which he adapted Plato's dialogue of that name to a new setting. When the Greek text disappeared for a time, Augustine learned his Plato from Cicero; and then he in turn preserved the tradition by defending political philosophy from the hostility of some of the early Church Fathers, who found it to be carnal, ungodly, and misleading. Plato and Aristotle, we should note, were kept alive by Muslims, beginning with al-Farabi (878–950), and Jews, above all Maimonides (1135–1204), both of whom also defended political philosophy from the suspicion that it did not accord with the divinely inspired law of their respective communities. Jewish and Muslim political and religious traditions are often considered not to be Western, and that view of them makes sense. But from the standpoint of the philosophical tradition, one may hold

---

CICERO (106–43 B.C.) was born into the equestrian rank in Rome. He trained in the law and studied philosophy in Greece before being elected to the consulate in 64. As consul, he defeated the conspiracy of Cataline and was hailed as a hero. Cicero was banished in 58, however, his property confiscated and his family harassed. After eighteen months in Greece, he was able to return to Rome and public life. Cicero sided with the aristocratic party of Pompey but was pardoned by Julius Caesar after Pompey's defeat in 48. Cicero retired to a life of philosophical leisure, but the assassination of Caesar in 44 brought him back into politics as a mentor to Caesar's heir, Octavian. In time, Octavian turned against him and Cicero was hunted down and murdered as he fled Italy.

that any nation having had contact with Greek philosophy or science belongs to the West. Certainly Muslim and Jewish philosophers were essential to that tradition not only for what they said but also for transmitting ancient philosophy to the medieval or modern West (in the political or geographical sense).

Augustine, like Plato, looked down on partisan politics. It was not that both men despised worldly goods or useful political solutions, but rather that they were concerned to emphasize the limitations of such goods and solutions. Augustine went so far as to say that kingdoms are nothing but grand larcenies, and ordinary larcenies nothing but small kingdoms. Alexander the Great's conquest of the world with a huge fleet is not essentially different from a pirate's robbery made with a single ship. No responsible citizen or statesman could take such a view, as by itself it might lead to despondency or despair, and perhaps it is not even true. But Augustine wanted to make the point that moral virtue, contrary to Aristotle's glowing picture, is always tainted with human self-interest, and always in need of God's grace. Just as for Plato the only true virtue is philosophic, so for Augustine, true virtue is Christian. But whereas philosophic virtue is accessible only to a few, Christian virtue is open to everyone (though some know it better), and it is an ever-present possibility not dependent on the political situation of the moment.

To explain this possibility, Augustine developed his famous doctrine of the two cities, the earthly city and the city of God. Neither is any particular city or nation (for example, the Jewish people); the earthly city is any city, and the city of God is the community of the worshippers of the true God. The latter exists in heaven but also exists on earth to the extent that men follow Christ. It is not utopian, a city only in speech like Plato's best regime in the *Republic*. Nor do the two cities necessarily conflict: they may be united

---

AUGUSTINE (354–430) was born in Roman North Africa. In his youth he proved an excellent student of the Latin classics, and at the age of 19 his philosophical interest was stirred upon reading Cicero. Torn between the noble ideals of that Roman thinker and his own disorderly erotic life, Augustine found solace for a time in the Manichean teaching of dualism. He set out for Italy at the age of 28 and secured a position in the imperial court at Milan. There, his spiritual crisis came to a head, and Augustine was converted to Christianity. He retired to a villa, where he wrote his first philosophical and theological works, often in the form of dialogues. Returning to North Africa, he was pressed into priestly service about 391 and consecrated bishop of Hippo in 395. From then, his primary responsibility was to care for the souls of the local Christian community, and his voluminous writings—scriptural commentaries, sermons, letters, and philosophical and theological treatises—were all written with that end in view. He died during the Visigoth siege of Carthage.

under a Christian prince. The earthly city, however, is tainted with original sin and lives according to the "flesh" (in the biblical sense). It is counteracted and perfected by the human conscience, the conscience to be found in all men, good and wicked, that awakens in the soul when men do wrong. Human partisanship arising from sin has its own correction, both natural and divine, in the conscience.

With Thomas Aquinas, we enter the millennium just passed, the one containing his great summation of the tradition (his books, the *Summa Theologiae* and the *Summa Contra Gentiles*, were summations; he also wrote commentaries on Aristotle and the Bible, among other things), and the great revolt of modern philosophers against the tradition. Thomas was canonized as a saint by the Catholic Church in 1323 and the study of his doctrine was enjoined by Pope Leo XIII in 1879. "Thomism," as it is known, acquired a special if not quite official status, though today in Catholic thought its reign is weakened and contested. Yet, despite its success, it was denounced by the bishop of Paris in 1277 soon after it first appeared.

The controversy arose from Thomas's introduction of Aristotle's philosophy, passed along from Arab philosophers, particularly Averroes (1126–1198). To the bishop it seemed that Aquinas and his cohort were denying or endangering the truth of Christian revelation by borrowing from—even relying on—a pagan philosopher (whose works were learned of from non-Christian philosophers who did the same). Is not philosophy, the activity of human reason, based on human vanity, on the vain presumption of the sufficiency of human reason without divine revelation? Aquinas answered that it is not. Nature, he thought, was created by God in such a way that its order can be understood by human reason unassisted by Christian revelation. Nature is open to philosophy, and its greatest knower happened to be the pagan Aristotle, whom Aquinas calls simply "the philosopher." Unassisted human reason cannot know everything that humans can know; it cannot know the greatest truths of the divinity of Christ and His promise of salvation. But just as God's grace adds to nature, Christian truth completes natural truth without changing it. Christians need not be wary of philosophy; they can welcome it without fear that it will lead necessarily to atheism or to belief in false gods like the Delphic oracle whom Socrates pretended to obey.

For politics, Aquinas expounded a doctrine of natural law that soon acquired authority as the greatest expression of that view. Natural law in political philosophy is not to be found in the Greeks but was first seen in Cicero's writings, where it is attributed, with some stretching, to the Stoics. Similar to the natural justice or natural right of which Plato and Aristotle spoke, it is not identical. Whereas natural justice takes effect through the regime, natural law sets the basis for regimes and so precedes the regime. Natural justice is more flexible, and therefore runs a greater risk of seeming relativistic than does natural law. In Aquinas's version, natural law, too, has a certain flexibility; it must always be applied, or promulgated, in human law. Aquinas spoke of natural justice as well as natural law, attempting perhaps to combine them. Yet on the whole Aquinas's natural law is stricter than Aristotle's natural justice, and consequently less supple politically. Aristotle did not speak of a

---

THOMAS AQUINAS (1225–1274) was born to a noble Italian family and he received his early education from Benedictine monks. While at university, he was attracted to a vigorous new order of mendicant clergy, the Dominicans, and he went to Paris and Cologne to study with the great Dominican scholar Albertus Magnus. From 1252 until his death, Aquinas would hold teaching positions at universities both in France and Italy. In 1257, he was created Doctor of Theology in the University of Paris. Aquinas lived an active life, advising popes, kings, and princes, publicly disputing both philosophical and theological questions, preaching, playing an active role in his order, and writing. He died in 1274 en route to the Ecumenical Council of Lyons.

conscience in all, nor of a universal natural inclination to virtue, as did Aquinas. In comparison with Aristotle, what Aquinas gains in universality he loses in political prudence. His political philosophy is necessarily affected, one could say endowed, by the superpolitical character of Christianity, which in other Christians, but not in him, produced indifference to worldly politics.

THE PERPETUAL REPUBLIC

WE TURN NOW to Niccolò Machiavelli (1469–1527), the first modern thinker. He was the first modern because he had the amazing ambition to bring politics, and with politics all other human problems, under a greater degree of human control than had ever before been thought possible. He launched a movement of modern philosophers who, despite their disagreements with him and even their disavowals of his influence, followed him in the essential point he set forth. From now on, politics would be less chancy, less subject to shifts of fortune, and human life would be better. More than that, Machiavelli indicated that an irreversible course of progress would be set in motion so that politics would never again regress to corruption and partisan excess. This new state of affairs he called the "perpetual republic," a remedy for political ills that he characteristically first denies and then affirms to be possible, leaving to the reader the job of seeing what he means. Machiavelli thought that men could have much greater power over events if they were "wised up," a teaching process known later, in the eighteenth century, as Enlightenment. This grand project has not worked out as intended—which we know simply from observing the horrifying totalitarian regimes that disfigured the twentieth century. Somehow the fruits of science in these regimes were poison to liberty. But even before this grievous spectacle, the Enlightenment was subjected to two great criticisms which I shall discuss presently, from Rousseau and from Nietzsche.

But ever since Machiavelli, the central idea expressed in modern political philosophy—agree with it or not—has been the focus of debate. Politics not only in the West but everywhere on earth has been dominated by Machiavelli's promise of "new modes and orders," of modernity, issued first in the two books he wrote containing, he said, "everything he knows"—*The Prince* and the *Discourses on Livy*.

It is thus of the utmost importance to understand what modernity is, how the moderns opposed the ancients (and the Christians, who in the moderns' view derived from the ancients), how modernity developed in stages, the history it experienced, and the crises it has suffered. Yet none of these matters are obvious in Machiavelli—as they are somewhat later in Francis Bacon (1561–1626) and Thomas Hobbes (1588–1679). Machiavelli lived during and participated in the Renaissance, a rebirth of the influence of the ancients and a time that could easily be seen as reactionary rather than progressive. He spoke of the ancients and moderns, but he called the moderns weak and supposed they could become strong only by imitating the ancients in politics, not only in humane letters as other Renaissance thinkers believed. Although Machiavelli opposed the utopian views of the Socratic tradition, referring to them as imaginary republics and principalities, with later modern philosophers he agreed that politics was the focus of human life. The modern revolution in political philosophy against the tradition was based partly on agreement with the tradition.

To imitate the ancients, Machiavelli chose the Romans rather than the Greeks, and he analyzed their actual politics as opposed to their political philosophy. For this purpose he wrote his *Discourses on Livy*, a loose commentary on the Roman historian Titus Livy. As you read along in that book, you realize that Machiavelli is gradually replacing Livy's analysis with his own; these are Machiavelli's Romans, not the Romans as they were, or as they appeared to themselves. At the same time you begin to see that the ancients were not so strong after all, for they lost out to the Christians—the ancient Romans succumbed to the modern Romans. Yet it was Christianity that Machiavelli accused as the cause of weakness in his own time. In a day when all feared the power of the Church, he was easily its boldest critic, or better to say, attacker. The Church caused weakness, he believed, by teaching men to despise worldly glory and to seek salvation in humble contemplation instead of manly virtue. Still, there must be some reason why the Christian Church was so powerful, some reason why the effeminate moderns could conquer the strong ancients. One source of power, perhaps, was

---

NICCOLÒ MACHIAVELLI (1469–1527) in his youth read extensively in Latin and Italian classics. The expulsion of the Medici in 1494 propelled Machiavelli into the office of secretary of the Florentine republic, a post he would hold from 1498 to 1512. He was an energetic and well-traveled statesman who was repeatedly dispatched as an envoy by the republic, for which he wrote many diplomatic despatches. In 1512, the Medici returned to power in Florence. Machiavelli was implicated in a conspiracy against them, was imprisoned and tortured, and released in 1513. Machiavelli's political career now appeared at an end, and he turned to writing, an occupation that brought him far greater fame than that of any of his patrons.

in Christian propaganda, the ability of Christians to take their message directly to peoples without having to conquer a country militarily as did the Muslims. Machiavelli wondered whether he might not adopt this method himself, and oppose Christian ends by Christian means. This was the germ of the Enlightenment, a conversion of peoples away from faith in God to faith in human control, led by philosophers (of the type we now call "intellectuals") and oriented against priests.

How does Machiavelli propose to improve permanently the control we humans exercise through politics? Machiavelli examines the partisanship of politics that was so important to Plato and Aristotle. He appreciates that Christianity tried to put an end to such partisanship with belief in God, who is above parties and directs human justice to an end above itself; but he notes that partisanship continues and that Christians actually inflame it by claiming that God is on their side—not above them, but behind them. Early in the *Discourses on Livy* Machiavelli looks at parties in Rome and Florence very differently than did Plato, Thucydides, and Aristotle. He pays no attention to the opinions expressed by partisans but instead turns to their underlying motives, or "humors," as he calls them, using a medical or psychological term relating to the body, not the soul. Rather than follow partisan opinions to what they imply for the best regime, he undercuts them, reducing their pretensions to the actual effects that result from their talk. This is what Machiavelli meant in *The Prince* when he spoke of seeking the "effectual truth" rather than imagined magnifications of fact. The strategy of reducing human pretensions to motives underlying and undercutting them was imitated by later modern thinkers, and is often called "reductionism."

The motives Machiavelli found were two opposed but not contrary humors: that of the few, or the princes, who desire to command or dominate; and that of the many, the people, who desire only not to *be* dominated. For Machiavelli, as opposed to Aristotle, there is no contest as to who should rule, but only a conflict between those who want to rule and those who do not want to be ruled. Neither side understands, or can be brought to understand, the other. Political men do not see why anyone could be satisfied with a life without glory, and nonpolitical types do not see the reason why they should bother. No justice can ever come about between two such humors, as the rulers always want too much and the ruled are never willing to concede enough. Obviously, then, rulers can rule only by concealing their rule from the ruled, only by a kind of fraud. Let's not go into the dirty details of Machiavelli's little tricks. It's enough to say that he has a "remedy" (his word) for the problem of partisanship as he has redefined it, a remedy in which justice has been abandoned and the common good newly understood as not including those few who on occasion may need to be murdered so as to keep everyone on his toes, ready to obey. We may be intrigued and impressed by Machiavelli, but I am obliged to say it would be wrong to approve of him. The real remedy he provides is a cold bath for those—most all of us at one time or another—who are guilty of complacent moralism and find it easy to condemn others and hard to examine themselves. But doesn't the Bible say some such thing?

POLITICAL SYSTEMS

THOMAS HOBBES (1588–1679) formalized Machiavelli; he put him in a formula, made him more universal, exact, and scientific, and took away his concern for great individuals and founding deeds. With Hobbes, the passion of modern thought for *theory* becomes visible and paramount. The ancients tried to consider things from all points of view and to consult all opinions; they tried to understand and they aimed for wisdom. Anyone who reads them now may question their relevance to today's issues, but one can hardly fail to learn from them unless one is entirely preoccupied with those issues. But the moderns produce theories; they have a project and aim for change or reform. They would rather be right according to their theories than wise without a theory. Their theories single out a single factor—for example, glory in Machiavelli and self-preservation in Hobbes—on the basis of which they fashion a "system" (a modern word) that is intended to effect a reform in human affairs. Rather than address the whole, as is required for wisdom, they look at things systematically, as prompted by their theory. Modern theories are deliberately incomplete. No one seeking to describe the whole of human life would say that self-preservation is the center of it, as do Hobbes and Locke; but they say it so as to get a grip on our problems and to find a solution.

Hobbes saw before him the problem of religious war in England among partisans of the Catholic Church, Anglican Church, and Protestant sects. The unity of Christendom under the medieval Church had collapsed, and Hobbes looked for a remedy that would prove more lasting than any mere compromise among the warring parties. He came up with a novel concept he called the "state of nature," a concept which revolutionized political thinking and still today remains the fundamental principle of modern life. Modern life is the life of individuals, which does not mean outstanding individuals, persons who by nature or character are distinguished from others in some striking way. Such persons do exist today, but they are overshadowed by abstract individuals who do not stand out but are said to be individual merely by being born human. The individual is abstracted from actual, everyday society (in which all kinds of inequalities exist due to age, experience, or capacity), and put in a state of nature in which all are stripped of such advantages and disadvantages and found to be equal. Hobbes never gave much of a proof that all men are equal, but he launched the assumption that they can be taken to be equal. The assumption is still unproven, but it has become immensely successful. It does not necessarily establish democracy, or at least not right away, but it gives every state a democratic tendency and a universal basis in man as man.

Hobbes himself was no democrat and he did not want a universal state. The devices he invented for avoiding the apparent consequences of assuming the existence of, or imagining, a state of nature have been almost as influential as the assumption itself. All men being equal in the state of nature, they would be rivals for the necessities of life; they would be in fear of one another, and they would fight. They would be willing if not eager to leave behind their universal equality and would consent to authorize a sovereign to govern in their name. Because the sovereign has been authorized by the people, he represents them and does not impose on them when he governs. "Representation" has a new sense because it now refers to the whole government, not merely to institutions like the medieval parliaments that connected

---

THOMAS HOBBES (1588–1679) was the son of an impoverished clergyman in Malmsbury. As to his birth, he liked to joke that his mother went into labor the day (April 5, 1588) when the Spanish Armada was approaching England, "so that fear and I were born twins together." Skilled in the classics, his first publication in 1629 was a translation of Thucydides. Avoiding the professions, he became secretary to William Cavendish, the Earl of Devonshire, and spent the rest of his life in the employ of that noble family or a related one, that of the Earl of Newcastle. He also served as secretary to Francis Bacon. Hobbes toured Europe as tutor to the son of Lord Cavendish and met leading statesmen and philosophers such as Galileo, Gassendi, and Descartes. Just after the Civil War began in 1642, he published *De Cive* ("On the Citizen") in Paris. This was the second of three political treatises, the first being *The Elements of Law* (finished in 1640 and not published until 1650), and the third, *Leviathan*, his most famous book, published in 1651. Among his other writings is an autobiography. He is described vividly in John Aubrey's *Brief Lives*.

the king (who was not authorized by the people) to the people. Thus is born government that owes its being, not merely its support, to the consent of the people. The people were not understood by Hobbes to be a working democracy—a government he disliked—and any distinctions within the people, such as nobles and commoners, owed their existence in his system to the decision of the sovereign, hence ultimately to the consent of the people. Still, whatever the sovereign decides the people must obey, because they have authorized the sovereign to act on their behalf. Sovereignty needs to be absolute. Any limitation of its power would in effect divide power against itself and return the people to the state of nature they had wished to escape.

There is reason behind this paradoxical system, which begins from complete liberty in the state of nature and moves to complete submission under the sovereign. Hobbes, like Machiavelli, wanted a permanent solution to the problem of religious partisanship. Whereas Machiavelli reduced partisan opinions to two humors underlying them, Hobbes took the reduction one step further and found one fundamental factor: the "passion to be relied upon," that is, fear. Fear is the universal motive in men, with priority over all other motives. To get anything you desire you must be alive,

Hobbes wishes to remind you. With self-preservation as the foundation on which to build, society will be both stronger and freer because it will no longer be subject to war begun by those who want to impose their piety on you. And while the ambitions of pious men are suppressed, so too is the stubbornness of the spirited and the courageous. Here Hobbes departs from Machiavelli, who had looked for princes to *inspire* fear. Hobbes looks for subjects who *feel* fear.

Hobbes's scheme was too extreme to work—too contrary to virtue and common sense. John Locke (1632–1704)

JOHN LOCKE (1632–1704) was the son of a Puritan landowner and attorney. He studied at Christ Church, Oxford, and later took a position as a tutor there in Greek, rhetoric, and philosophy. He also practiced medicine. Always circumspectly interested in politics, Locke in 1667 became private secretary to Ashley Cooper, later the Earl of Shaftesbury, a leader of the Protestant party in the political intrigues of Restoration England. In this capacity Locke drafted a constitution for the Carolina colony in America, in which Shaftesbury held an interest. His patron's changing political fortunes also determined Locke's. In 1675, Locke took the opportunity of Shaftesbury's fall from the chancellorship to retire to France for study; Shaftesbury's return to power as a privy councilor in 1679 brought Locke back to London. Suspected of complicity in plots against the government, Locke fled to Amsterdam in 1683 and spent the next half decade in study and writing, returning after the Glorious Revolution. Almost all of the writings which would bring him fame appeared after 1690; religious controversy in particular became his chief concern in his last years. Beyond his "civil" works, his main philosophical book is *An Essay Concerning Human Understanding*.

took its basis, the state of nature, and fashioned a more regular, constitutional system that retained the modern non-partisan intent in a new design. Locke remade Hobbes's absolute sovereignty, not abandoning it but making it compatible with constitutional checks and limited government. From the Whig party in the English Civil War he borrowed the idea of legislative supremacy, and from the Tories he took their insistence on kingly prerogative, now transformed into a strong executive. Both the principles and the political institutions in Locke's constitution resemble ours, and in our passage through the tradition of political philosophy, for the first time we feel at home. Not only do we recognize the broad outline of the modern constitution, but we also come upon Locke's argument for private property, which is essential to the modern economy, and his argument for religious toleration, the beginning of the modern practice of free speech. Locke has something for both conservatives and liberals in his balanced system, and he moderates Hobbes's ignoble reliance on fear, extending it to a more general, neutral sense of *uneasiness* in man. Our uneasiness makes us worry over our security, and sometimes spurs us to stand up for our rights and even fight for our liberty. A certain degree of the spiritedness in man, of which

Plato and Machiavelli made so much, reenters Locke's politics, enabling it to inspire the American Revolution of 1776, as well as lay down that revolution's principles.

Yet the point of our tour though political philosophy is not to relax when we have reached something familiar. For one thing, we have now *placed* Locke, and therefore ourselves, in a definite situation. He is part of a movement of rebellion known as "modernity," and so are we. It must not be forgotten that America—the "regime" America, as Aristotle defines that word—began with a revolution, and one not merely for Americans but ostensibly on behalf of all mankind. It must also not be forgotten that in comparison to the revolutions that followed, this was a moderate one, and perhaps for that reason it has proved more lasting. The moderation, I would say, consists in not seeking a perfect substitute for the virtue that the ancients (variously) described, but in continuing to leave opportunity for virtue. America has been more successful than other regimes by not trying to guarantee success. When you rely on virtue to appear, you may not get it. Enlightened statesmen, as *The Federalist* said, may not always be at the helm. But when you do not rely on virtue, you have to make a new man. This is the idea to which Jean-Jacques Rousseau

(1712-1778) gave birth. It was not an idea he would precisely accept as his own, but it was his bastard.

THE BOURGEOIS SELF
ॐ

IF LOCKE PLEASES US with his liberal constitutionalism, Rousseau makes us aware of its difficulties and its rivals. Rousseau focuses on the "self" that is behind the Hobbes-Locke notion of self-preservation: he says that Hobbes and Locke take the self for granted and do not examine it properly. They tried to reach the state of nature that preexisted society, but, he says, they "did not go back far enough." They say that the state of nature is warlike and competitive, but this can be so only if the self (which they wish to substitute for the soul) is anxious about other people, only if it is *social*. If you are selfish, you are in a sense social—because you are not satisfied with your self but concerned with what others get, say, or think. You are divided within yourself; you are not *one* self. Part of you is real and authentic; part of you is controlled by the need to please others. You are a *bourgeois*, a name Rousseau made a term of reproach for a wide range of conflicting sins, including power-seeking, love of money, risk-averseness, and desire for respectability—all of which issue, in Rousseau's view, from fear.

In his politics, Rousseau proposed to turn the unattractive bourgeoisie into citizens with a simple but paradoxical theoretical twist that would give selfish individuals a general will. This would be "as it were" a change of human nature, hence almost the new man I spoke of. They would "alienate" their particular rights to the collectivity, and by the very act of alienating create that collectivity together with a general will to guide it. This almost-new man would live in a new society equipped with a general will enabling it to come to decisions without having to deal with partisan or selfish divisions. Rousseau attacked the modern idea

---

JEAN-JACQUES ROUSSEAU (1712–1778), the son of a Swiss watchmaker, left Geneva at the age of 16 to find his fortune. In Turin he converted to Roman Catholicism and lived for ten years in the service of a "benefactress," Mme. de Warens. In the 1740s, he moved to Paris where he composed a ballet and a light opera and became familiar with the "enlightened" ideas of the *philosophes*. He achieved celebrity in 1750 with the publication of his *Discourse on the Arts and Sciences*, an essay emphatically contradicting the optimistic views of the Enlightenment. Rousseau's private life was always irregular. He fathered several bastard children by an illiterate serving-maid and abandoned them all in foundling homes. He was banished from France after the publication of *Emile* in 1762, and briefly spent time in England at the invitation of the philosopher David Hume. He eventually returned to France, always continuing to write. He died in 1778 and his remains were entombed at the Pantheon by the revolutionary French government.

of nonpartisanship at its source, the fearful self, but far from abandoning the idea, he extended it, radicalized it.

After Rousseau the attempt to create a new man began in earnest. Immanuel Kant (1724–1804) was a factor in the movement even though he was a revolutionary in thought rather than deed. Somehow he managed to welcome the French Revolution and its promise to create a new man while frowning on the violent and illegal means the Revolution eagerly embraced. Kant founded a new morality based on the "categorical imperative," as he called it, the principle that one should act only on the basis of universal laws instead of particular obligations or private motivations. With this device, morality is made distinct from the tendencies of human nature and the facts of a particular situation, which might give us a bias toward our particular selves or others like us in some particular aspect. Kant provides the ultimate nonpartisan morality; it is not even partisan in favor of human beings (except as rational beings), let alone more familiar sources of bias such as being a male, white, Anglo-Saxon Protestant. Kant's politics is driven by his moral philosophy to establish republics that would be impartial toward their own peoples and peace-seeking in international affairs: "perpetual peace," he said!

Rousseau began the great surge of hostility toward the bourgeoisie that coursed through the nineteenth and twentieth centuries in modern thought. Even though Kant approved of bourgeois commerce (because trading nations are more peaceful), he added to Rousseau's attack by denying any title of morality to the interested motives characteristic of the bourgeoisie. Others went further. Karl Marx (1818–1883) formulated a theory of a communist society that would inevitably come into being in the near future as a result of the operation of "iron laws" of economic necessity. The new communist man would be a well-rounded individual, no longer a victim of the tyranny of the division of labor which in bourgeois society compels men to lead narrow lives in one-sided roles. Friedrich Nietzsche (1844–1900) took the other way to attack the bourgeois produced by modern liberalism. Whereas Marx saw the bourgeois man to be selfish, Nietzsche showed him to be petty and ignoble. Both complaints have some truth to them, and both have fueled rage and enmity toward the bourgeoisie, Marx on the Left and Nietzsche on the Right. Nietzsche looked to a new man, a "Superman" in the future, who by his proud creativity would overcome the ghastly herdlike conformism of democratic mass man, now hardly a man—

indeed, the "last man." Disgust with the bourgeoisie became the theme of Western culture as society divided into those who made money and those (on both Left and Right) who despised money-making. The most important novel of the nineteenth century was perhaps Gustave Flaubert's *Madame Bovary* (1857), a story about a woman who commits adultery because her husband is boring. The reader is led to accept her misdeed and sympathize with her because her boring husband is bourgeois. She had good reason to be bored. Boredom is a modern affliction that comes with modern rationality. As life is made more predictable and secure, it becomes mediocre, uninteresting, and lacking in risk or challenge.

In sum, with Rousseau and those he influenced, modern thought turns against its own creation, against itself. But in doing so, modern thought does not for the most part reconsider the wisdom of its major project. It does not wonder whether it was a mistake to seek greater rational control over events and for this purpose to invent theories that oversimplify human nature. Of course, as we have seen even in this quick summary, there are many modern thinkers, and they usually disagree with one another's diagnoses and remedies. And there were thinkers who wanted to return, with modifications, to the ancients, such as Shaftesbury (1621-1683), Lessing (1729-1781), and Goethe (1749-1832). But these were, if not ignored, certainly not followed. There was also a return to nature in nineteenth-century romanticism, in art and literature as well as philosophy—but not to the ordered, intelligible nature of classical political philosophy. The romantics set nature against reason, which (following Rousseau) they regarded as petty, calculating, and confining, too limited ever to reach the heights of the sublime.

Nietzsche followed the romantic criticism to greater depths, reasoning his way to a more profound rejection of reason. He is responsible for the kind of animus against science that one sees today among the "postmoderns." Like Nietzsche, they regard science as motivated not by the desire to know, that is, by a scientific motive, but by a pre-scientific desire for power. Science can enslave us as well as liberate us. How obvious! How could we have missed that point? But the postmoderns, as their name indicates, have no positive alternative or supplement to science. They are too attached to the power and comforts of science to reject it, and they content themselves with biting the hand that feeds them. The little virtue they show in their complaints against science never rises to a recognition of the greatness of virtue. The best philosopher of the postmoderns is Martin Heidegger (1889–1976), and if you read his powerful works, you will see the difference between power and greatness.

Thus, the tendency of modern thought is to try to improve on itself and not to question itself. Even the greatest critics of modernity, Rousseau and Nietzsche, end by radicalizing, not moderating, the ambition of modernity. Rousseau said that the bourgeois self was divided (between the *self* and the *self-for-others*), but he went on to divide it further and then to attempt in several ways to patch over the split. Nietzsche said that man used the power of science to repress his own will to life, and then proceeded to seek salvation in this very will to power. What the moderns did

---

GEORG WILHELM FRIEDRICH HEGEL (1770–1831) was born in Stuttgart and educated in the Lutheran theological faculty at Tübingen. After graduation, he served as a tutor to families in Bern and Frankfurt, until 1801, when he took up a university post at Jena. In 1807 he published the *Phenomenology of Spirit*, but Napoleon's invading troops closed the university, and he was forced briefly to find employment editing a newspaper in Bamberg. Then, from 1808 until 1816, Hegel served as headmaster of the "Gymnasium" in Nuremberg, and in 1818 he was named to the chair of philosophy in the University of Berlin. There he lectured until his death during an outbreak of cholera. His writings are divided into treatises such as *The Philosophy of Right* and transcriptions of his lectures such as *The Philosophy of History*.

not attempt was to put reason and nature together, as did the ancients, so that reason sees both the greatness and the limitations of human beings. So we are left as we are now: rather small creatures with too much power. We have simultaneously belittled ourselves and empowered ourselves.

THE HISTORICAL TURN
᷾

INSTEAD OF RETURNING to nature in the classical sense, modern thinkers turned to history. In history you learn facts; you don't study natures. A fact is how things have turned out; nature is about how things have to be. Plato and Aristotle thought that facts come and go, but nature remains; nature is what should be studied. It was Machiavelli who first put fact to the fore, in his idea of the effectual truth. A fact is something that cannot be disputed. You must adjust to facts; they don't adjust to you. Facts speak for themselves. The same is not quite true of nature, and the difference is that the nature of a thing is often not easy to see and so seems to be a matter of opinion. You can see, for example, that you have lost a battle, but whether you deserve to lose is arguable, and from the standpoint of the fact, useless. Machiavelli's embrace of fact laid the basis for the nineteenth century's turn to history. Both fact and history have the nonpartisan advantage always sought by modernity: they cannot be argued with. Yet somehow, despite the assurance of all the experts that argument is pointless, we continue to argue. G. W. F. Hegel (1770–1831) distinguished mere fact from history, or from what he called World History. He was the master of the philosophy of history. Rather than let fact silence reason, he tried to infuse reason into fact; he saw the "march of Reason" in the facts of World History. World History, he tried to show, developed in "dialectical" stages until the Rational State was perfected—which by good chance (so I say) turned out to be the very state of Prussia in which Hegel was living. Here was the end (in the sense of the completion) of history: a state without parties in which there is nothing fundamental left to dispute. Yet as soon as the rational state was announced, everybody—Marx and Nietzsche in the forefront—scrambled to dispute it. Even as Hegel was writing, Tocqueville reproved the sort of democratic history that subjects human events to impersonal forces over which men have no control and that levels mankind to a herd of impotent individuals.

Peaceable liberal democracies, for whom wars over

religion are now inconceivable, still have parties—the liberals and conservatives we know so well. Actually, we would know them better if we studied John Stuart Mill (1806–1873) and Edmund Burke (1729–1797), the political philosophers who explain each the best. Make sure you read both Mill and Burke, not just the one you like. Mill argues for liberty and also for progress toward liberty. His difficulty is that progress requires enlightenment and the gradual defeat of prejudice—whereas liberty requires openness to all opinions, including prejudiced ones. What should a good liberal do for a conservative, teach him to think better or let him be as he is? Here is a conundrum always present to liberals.

FRIEDRICH NIETZSCHE (1844–1900) was born in a small town near Leipzig, the grandson of two Lutheran pastors. As a Gymnasium student, he became an enthusiastic follower of the Romantic composer Richard Wagner. At university, Nietzsche studied classical philology and quickly established an academic reputation. His philosophical interest was sparked when he happened upon a copy of Schopenhauer in a bookstore. Then, at the age of 24, he was offered a university chair in classical philology at Basel. For the next thirteen years, he worked as a conscientious professor in this provincial city. His books met with mixed reviews. Always in poor health, suffering from migraines, he resigned from Basel in 1879. For the next ten years he led an irregular life, traveling incessantly across south-central Europe and writing his major philosophical works. Finally, in 1889 he experienced a mental breakdown, from which he never recovered. He spent his remaining years as an invalid in the care of his mother and sister.

Then what about conservatives, are they better off? Burke opposed the French Revolution because it attempted to remake society according to a rational plan instead of letting it grow, spontaneously or by prudent adjustment, into a more convenient arrangement. Burke opposed that revolution as soon as he got word of it, and he correctly— amazingly—foresaw that it would lead to terror (Robespierre) and dictatorship (Napoleon). Still, when these things have occurred, what is a good conservative to do? Should he try to go back to the Old Regime before the revolution, which would be a disturbing counter-revolution, or should he adjust to the new status quo, in which case he compromises his conservative principle? This state of indecision between *going back* and *going slow* is the characteristic dilemma of the conservative, visible in every issue today. I leave it to you to decide which party is better, or which is worse (most partisans begin from what they don't like). You may conclude that the argument doesn't matter, but please don't suppose you can make it go away.

THIS IS NOT the only possible guide to political philosophy. I could have given it a theme different from that of partisanship, and of course there are several (but not many) interpretations of the nature and history of political philosophy. This guide is not intended for other professors, so it is not equipped with footnotes. I have written it to tell you what I really think (up to a point), but that is less important than the fact that it contains some of the most valuable information there is.

BIBLIOGRAPHY

BELOW ARE LISTED books from the authors I have discussed, in the translations I think the best (some of them are my own). If you want to become an advanced student of political philosophy, you should learn the original languages of these texts. Failing that—and who wants to wait to read Plato until he has learned Greek?—you should choose a literal translation done by someone who respects the thought of the author as opposed to someone who considers himself superior to this rather confused fellow.

Plato (427–347 B.C.). *The Republic of Plato*, trans. Allan Bloom; *Laws*, trans. Thomas Pangle; *Apology of Socrates*, in *Four Texts on Socrates*, trans. Thomas West and Grace Starry West.

Aristotle (384–322 B.C.). *The Politics*, trans. Carnes Lord; *Nicomachean Ethics*, trans. Hippocrates G. Apostle.

Thucydides (C.460–C. 400 B.C.). *History of the Peloponnesian War*, trans. R. Crawley.

Cicero (106–43 B.C.). *De re publica*, trans. C. W. Keyes (Loeb edition).

Augustine (354–430). *The City of God*, trans. Marcus Dods.

Al-Farabi (ca. 878–950). *The Political Regime*, in *Medieval Political Philosophy*, ed. Ralph Lerner and Muhsin Mahdi.

Moses **Maimonides** (1135–1204). *The Guide for the Perplexed*, trans. Shlomo Pines. Intro. by Leo Strauss.

Thomas **Aquinas** (1225–1274). *On Law, Morality, and Politics* (excerpts), ed. William P. Baumgarth and Richard J. Regan, S. J.

Niccolò **Machiavelli** (1469–1527). *The Prince*, trans. Harvey C. Mansfield; *Discourses on Livy*, trans. Harvey C. Mansfield and Nathan Tarcov.

Francis **Bacon** (1561–1626). *New Atlantis.*

Thomas **Hobbes** (1588–1679). *Leviathan.*

John **Locke** (1632–1704). *Two Treatises of Government*; *A Letter Concerning Toleration.*

Jean-Jacques **Rousseau** (1712–1778). *The Discourses and Other Early Political Writings,* trans. Victor Gourevitch; *On* *the Social Contract*, trans. Roger Masters.

Immanuel **Kant** (1724–1804). *Perpetual Peace and Other Essays*, trans. Ted Humphrey.

Edmund **Burke** (1729–1797). *Reflections on the Revolution in France*; *An Appeal from the New to the Old Whigs*.

G. W. F. **Hegel** (1770–1831). *The Philosophy of Right*, trans. T. M. Knox; *The Philosophy of History*, trans. J. Sibree.

Alexis de **Tocqueville** (1805–1859). *Democracy in America*, trans. Harvey C. Mansfield and Delba Winthrop.

John Stuart **Mill** (1806–1873). *On Liberty*; *Considerations on Representative Government*.

Karl **Marx** (1818–1883). *The Marx-Engels Reader*, ed. Robert Tucker.

Friedrich **Nietzsche** (1844–1900). *The Use and Abuse of History*, trans. Adrian Collins; *Beyond Good and Evil*, trans. Walter Kaufmann.

Martin **Heidegger** (1889–1976). *An Introduction to Metaphysics*, trans. Ralph Manheim; *Being and Time*, trans. Joan Stambaugh.

EMBARKING ON A LIFELONG PURSUIT OF KNOWLEDGE?

Take Advantage of These New Resources & a New Website

The ISI Guides to the Major Disciplines are part of the Intercollegiate Studies Institute's (ISI) **Student Self-Reliance Project**, an integrated, sequential program of educational supplements designed to guide students in making key decisions that will enable them to acquire an appreciation of the accomplishments of Western civilization.

Developed with fifteen months of detailed advice from college professors and students, these resources provide advice in course selection and guidance in actual coursework. The Project elements can be used independently by students to navigate the existing university curriculum in a way that deepens their understanding of our Western intellectual heritage. As indicated below, the Project's integrated components will answer key questions at each stage of a student's education.

What are the strengths and weaknesses of the most selective schools?
Choosing the Right College directs prospective college students to the best and worst that top American colleges have to offer.

What is the essence of a liberal arts education?
A Student's Guide to Liberal Learning introduces students to the vital connection between liberal education and political liberty.

What core courses should every student take?
A Student's Guide to the Core Curriculum instructs students in building their own core curricula, utilizing electives available at virtually every university, and discusses how to identify and overcome contemporary political biases in those courses.

How can students learn from the best minds in their major fields of study?
Student Guides to the Major Disciplines introduce students to overlooked and misrepresented classics, facilitating work within their majors. Guides currently available assess the fields of literature, philosophy, U.S. history, economics, political philosophy, and the study of history generally.

Which great modern thinkers are neglected?
The Library of Modern Thinkers introduces students to great minds who have contributed to the literature of the West and who are neglected or denigrated in today's classroom. Figures in this series include Robert Nisbet, Eric Voegelin, Wilhelm Röpke, Ludwig von Mises, Michael Oakeshott, Andrew Nelson Lytle, and many more.

In order to address the academic problems faced by every student in an ongoing manner, a new website, **www.collegeguide.org**, was recently launched. It offers easy access to unparalleled resources for making the most of one's college experience, and it features an interactive component that will allow students to pose questions about academic life on America's college campuses.

These features make ISI a one-stop organization for serious students of all ages. Visit **www.isi.org** or call **1-800-526-7022** and consider adding your name to the 50,000-plus ISI membership list of teachers, students, and professors.